WACO McLENNAN COUNTY LIBRARY
1717 AUSTIN AVE.
WACO, TX 76701

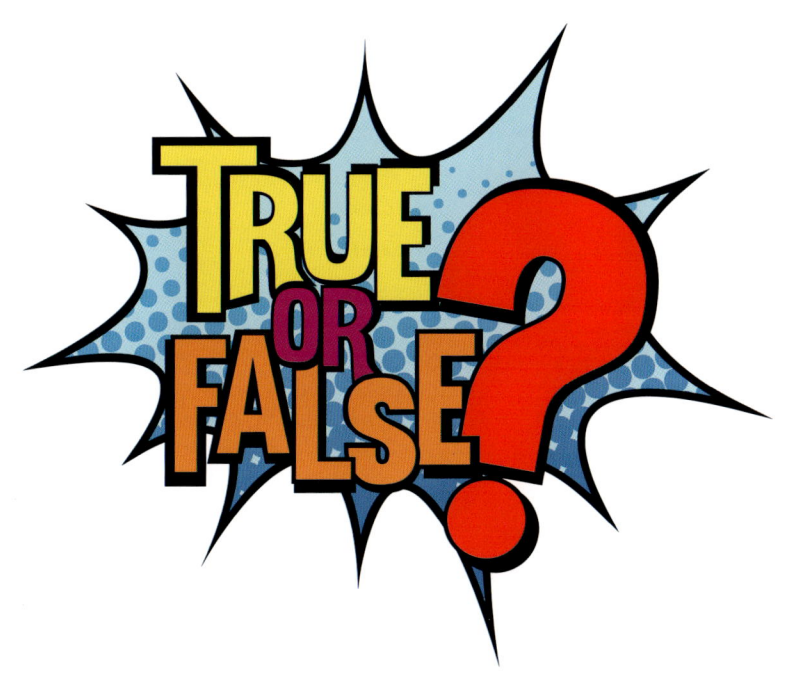

World Book, Inc.
180 North LaSalle Street
Suite 900
Chicago, Illinois 60601
USA

Copyright © 2019 (print and e-book) World Book, Inc.
All rights reserved.

This volume may not be reproduced in whole or in part in any form without prior written permission from the publisher.

WORLD BOOK and the GLOBE DEVICE are registered trademarks or trademarks of World Book, Inc.

For information about other "True or False?" titles, as well as other World Book print and digital publications, please go to www.worldbook.com.

For information about other World Book publications, call 1-800-WORLDBK (967-5325).

For information about sales to schools and libraries, call 1-800-975-3250 (United States) or 1-800-837-5365 (Canada).

Library of Congress Cataloging-in-Publication Data for this volume has been applied for.

True or False?
ISBN: 978-0-7166-3761-5 (set, hc.)

Ghosts
ISBN: 978-0-7166-3765-3 (hc.)

Also available as:
ISBN: 978-0-7166-3775-2 (e-book, ePUB3)

Printed in China by RR Donnelley,
Guangdong Province
1st printing May 2019

# Staff

## Executive Committee

President
Geoff Broderick

Vice President, Finance
Donald D. Keller

Vice President, Marketing
Jean Lin

Vice President, International
Maksim Rutenberg

Vice President, Technology
Jason Dole

Director, Human Resources
Bev Ecker

## Editorial

Director, New Print
Tom Evans

Writers
Madeline King
Shawn Brennan

Editor
Shawn Brennan

Librarian
S. Thomas Richardson

Manager, Contracts and Compliance
(Rights and Permissions)
Loranne K. Shields

Manager, Indexing Services
David Pofelski

## Digital

Director, Digital Product Development
Erika Meller

Digital Product Manager
Jonathan Wills

## Graphics and Design

Senior Art Director
Tom Evans

Senior Visual Communications Designer
Melanie Bender

Media Editor
Rosalia Bledsoe

## Manufacturing/Production

Manufacturing Manager
Anne Fritzinger

Production Specialist
Curley Hunter

Proofreader
Nathalie Strassheim

# TRUE OR FALSE?

# GHOSTS

WORLD BOOK

www.worldbook.com

# True or False?

A ghost is a spirit of a dead person that visits the living.

# TRUE!

Some people think that a dead person's spirit comes back to the living world.

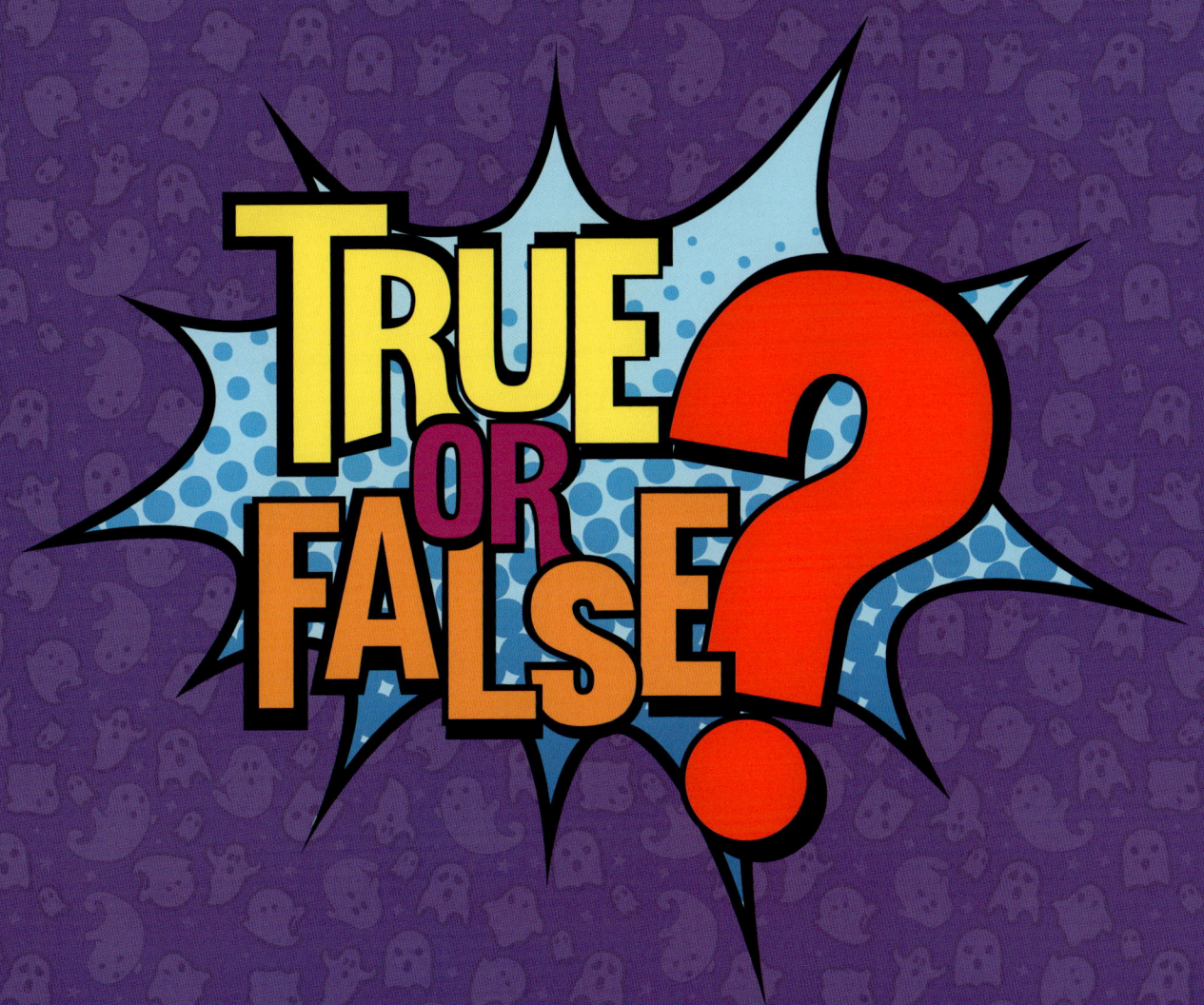

**People sometimes picture a ghost as a white, sheet-draped figure with a head and arms but no feet or legs.**

# TRUE OR FALSE?

**There is scientific proof that ghosts exist.**

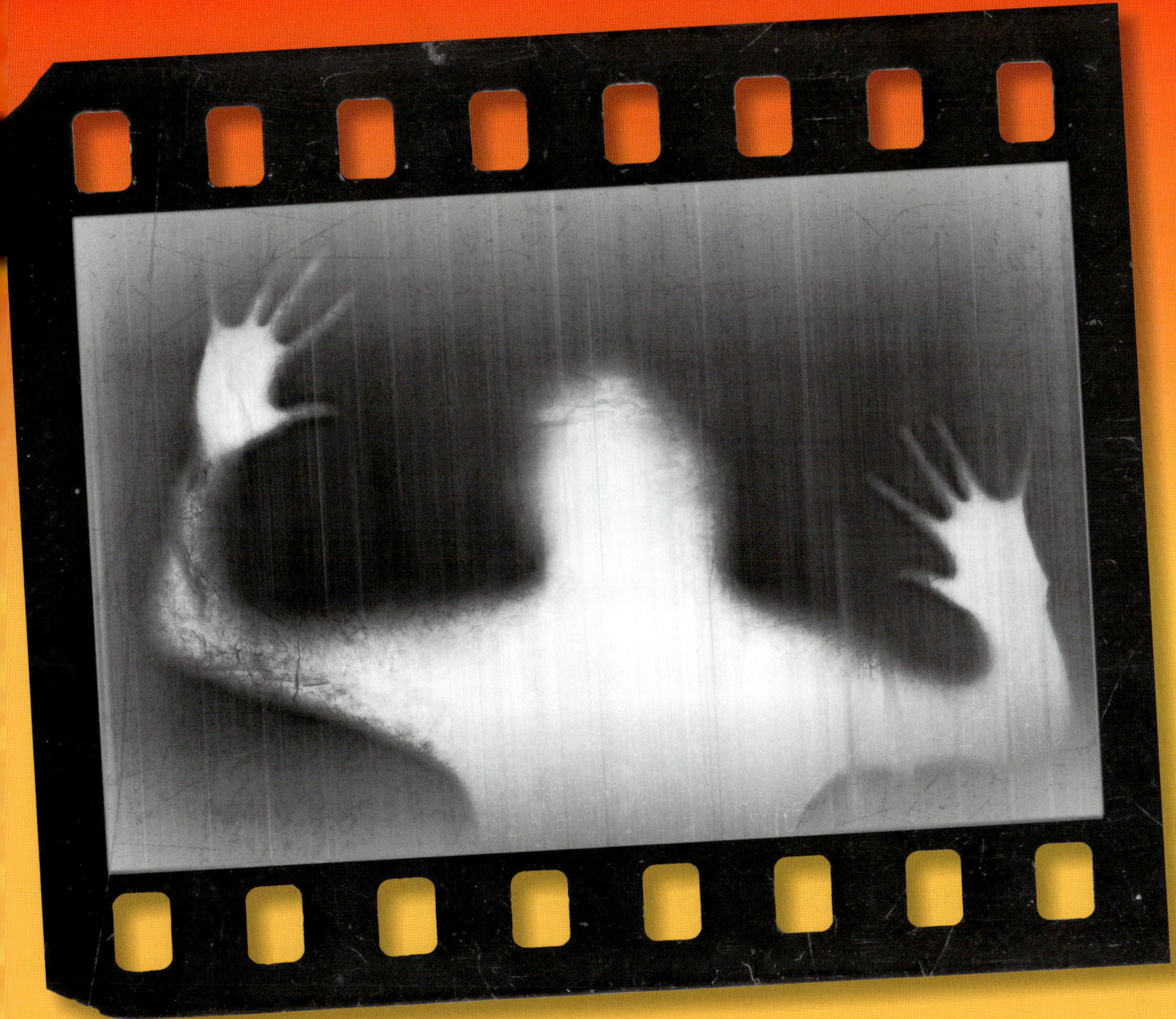

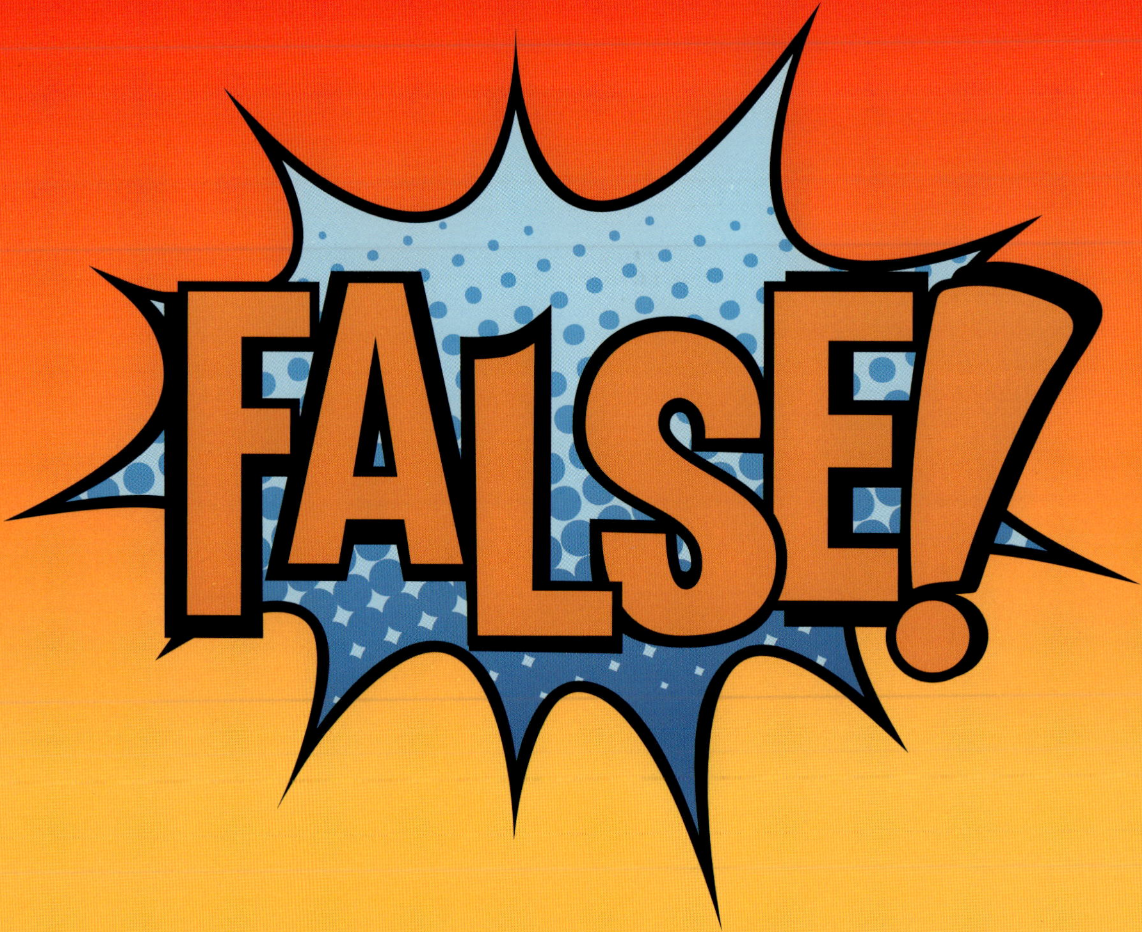

# FALSE!

There is no scientific proof that ghosts actually exist. But many people believe they have seen or heard these spirits.

This idea probably came from the practice of burying the dead wrapped inside a cloth called a *shroud*. Some people think that the dead still wear their shrouds when they return as ghosts. Did that creepy clothesline say "Boo?!"

# True or False?

All ghost stories portray ghosts as spiteful spirits who harm people.

There are stories of ghosts who harm people. But there are also stories about ghosts who help people. In Charles Dickens's story *A Christmas Carol,* the ghost Jacob Marley helps the main character, Ebenezer Scrooge, become a better person.

**TRUE!**

Maybe a ghost will ask for all of your Halloween candy. That would certainly give you a fright!

# True or False?

Many people claim that the ghost of Abraham Lincoln, who died tragically, sometimes appears at the White House, where he lived as president.

# TRUE!

Lincoln's ghost reportedly has been seen roaming around the White House by American first ladies Grace Coolidge, Eleanor Roosevelt, and Lady Bird Johnson, as well as by British Prime Minister Winston Churchill, Queen Wilhelmina of the Netherlands, and others. Honest, Abe!

# TRUE OR FALSE?

**If you are a Danish person who believes in ghosts, be afraid! *BE VERY AFRAID!***

# FALSE!

If you believe in the *gjenganger (YEHN gawng ehr)*, you'd better NOT be afraid! According to Danish mythology, the gjenganger is the spirit of a person who was laid to rest but is not at peace. It returns to its family to haunt them, feeding off their fear!

# True or False?

All ghost stories are about the spirits of living things.

There are many versions of a famous legend about a ghost ship called the *Flying Dutchman*. The most common story involves the sighting of a phantom ship as it attempts to sail around the Cape of Good Hope in Africa. However, the captain has been cursed and his crew consists of dead men.

The ship never reaches port and is doomed to sail on eternally. The English poet Samuel Taylor Coleridge based his poem "The Rime of the Ancient Mariner" (1798) on the legend. The German composer Richard Wagner adapted the story into his opera *The Flying Dutchman* (1843).

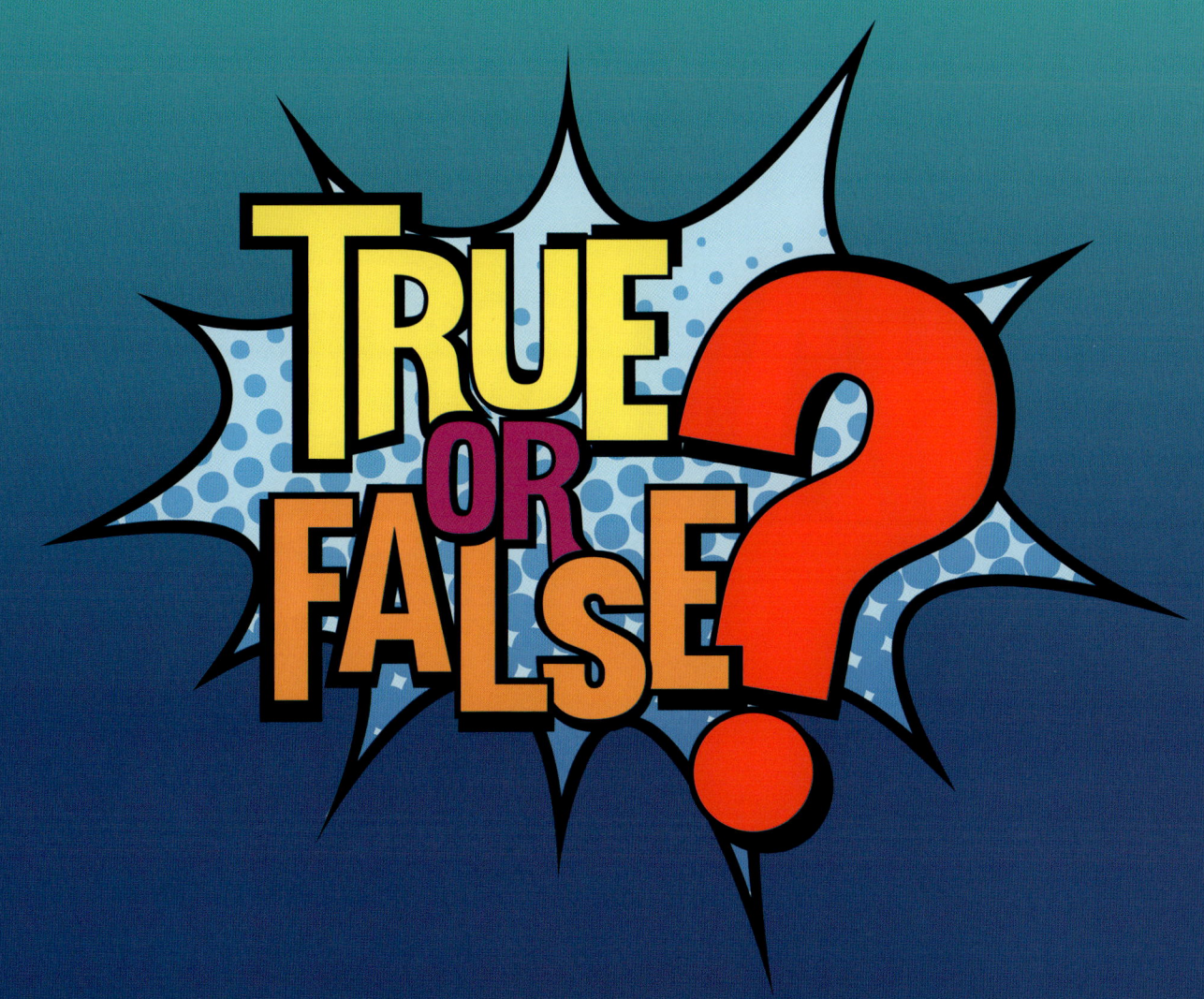

The American author Shirley Jackson based her famous novel *The Haunting of Hill House* (1959) on her own house.

Jackson was inspired by a photo of a haunted-looking California house she had seen in a magazine. Her mother later identified the house as one built by the author's own great-great-grandfather! He had been an architect who had built some of San Francisco's oldest buildings. How's that for a creepy coincidence?!

# TRUE OR FALSE?

There are real-life professional ghostbusters.

**Paranormal investigators, or professional ghost hunters, operate in places around the world. They use a variety of electronic devices, including thermometers, cameras, and audio recorders, to pick up ghostly activity.**

# True or False?

**Thomas Edison wanted to be a ghost hunter.**

44

**The great American inventor expressed an interest in developing a "spirit phone" that would record the voices of the dead.**

# TRUE OR FALSE?

Romania is home to the most haunted forest in the world.

# TRUE!

Hoia Baciu *(HOY uh BAH choo)* Forest in Cluj-Napoca *(KLOOZH nah POH kah)*, Romania, is known as the "world's most haunted forest." Visitors claim to feel like they are being watched.

They also claim to see ghosts and unidentified flying objects (UFO's) in the area. (The forest also happens to be located in Transylvania, the main site of the legend about the vampire Dracula!)

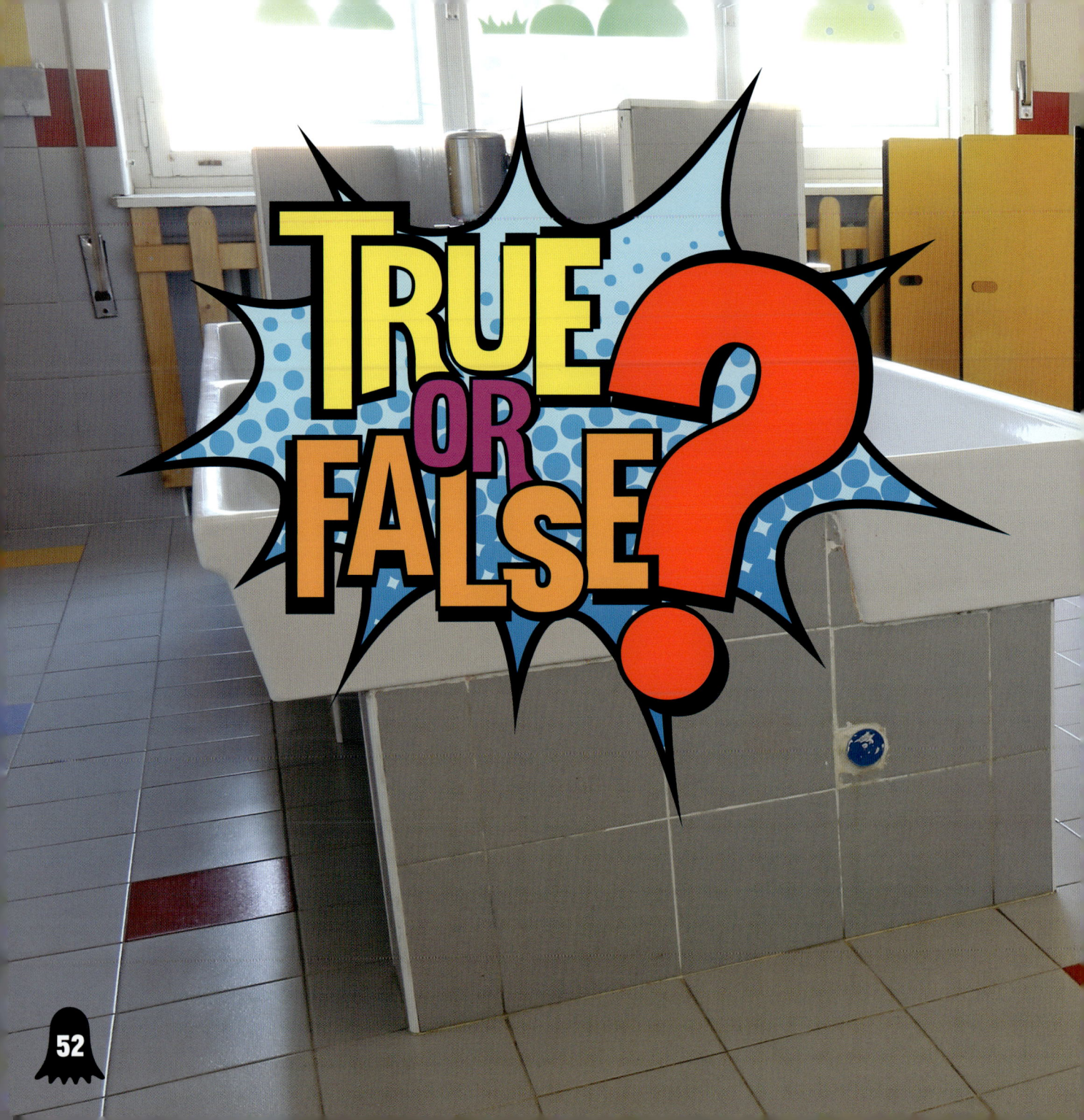

**In Japanese folklore, there are stories about ghosts who appear in bathrooms.**

# TRUE!

One famous ghost story tells of a young girl named Hanako-san *(hah nah koh sahn)* who haunts school bathrooms. Legend has it that she appears in the third-floor girls' bathroom in the third stall. Some people think she just wants to make friends. Others think she wants to drag students down the toilet! It's enough to make you flush with fear!

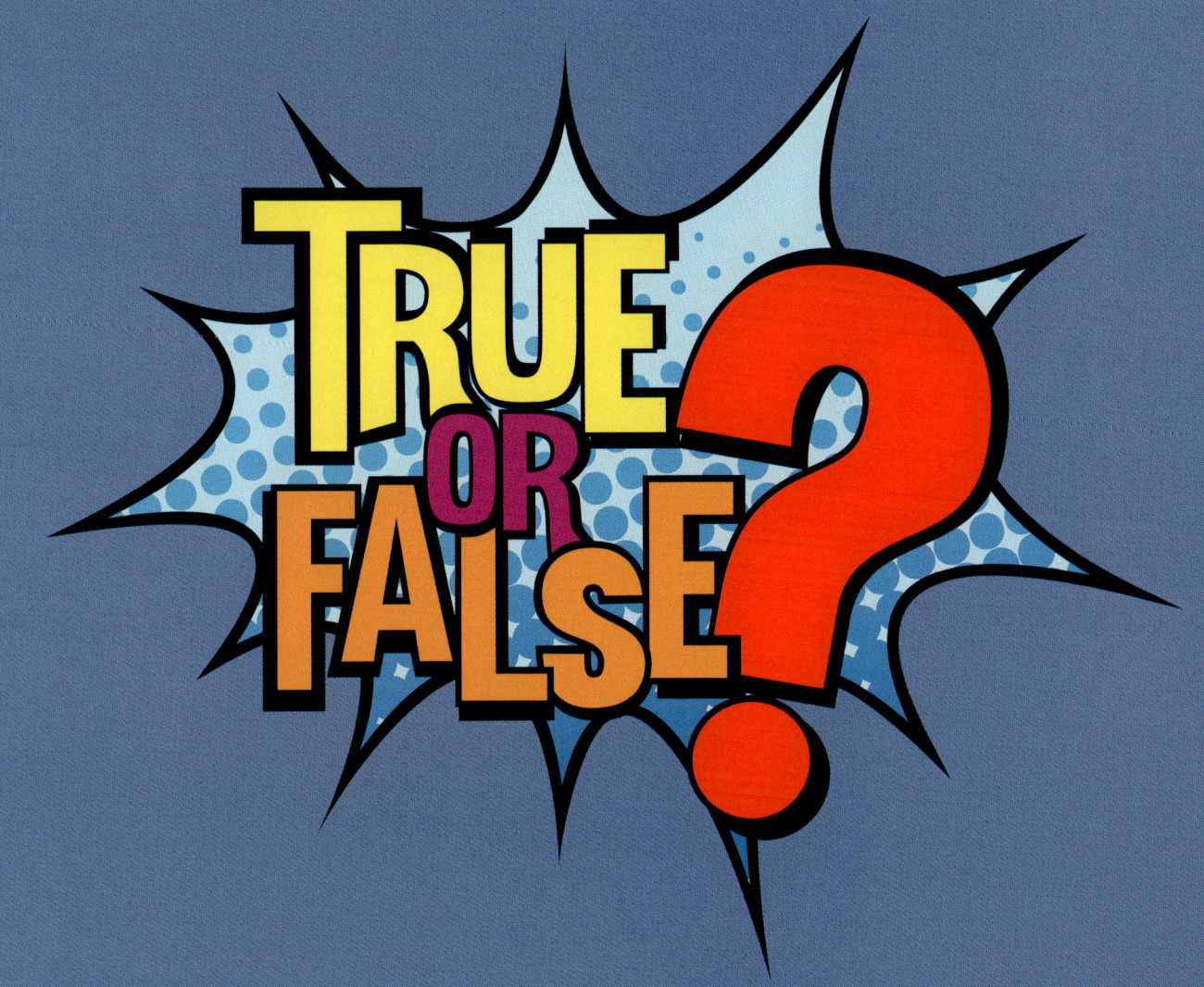

In Scandinavia, there is a ghost who represents the Black Death.

The Black Death was a deadly disease that struck Asia and Europe in the 1300's. The Black Death was actually a disease called plague. By about 1400, the Black Death had killed around 25 million Europeans. The ghost, described as an ugly, shriveled old woman, is called Pesta. If she comes to your house with a rake, some family members will live. But, if she comes with a broom: *TOTAL DISASTER!*

# True or False?

In the American Southwest, many children hear stories about a ghost who haunts kitchens.

**But many children of the American Southwest DO hear stories about *La Llorona (lah yoh ROH nah)*, or "the weeping woman." Storytellers describe her as a mother whose children drowned long ago. Her crying ghost continues to look for them. According to legend, she wanders near rivers and lakes and frightens people who meet her. Parents sometimes tell their children this story to discourage them from going near dangerous waters.**

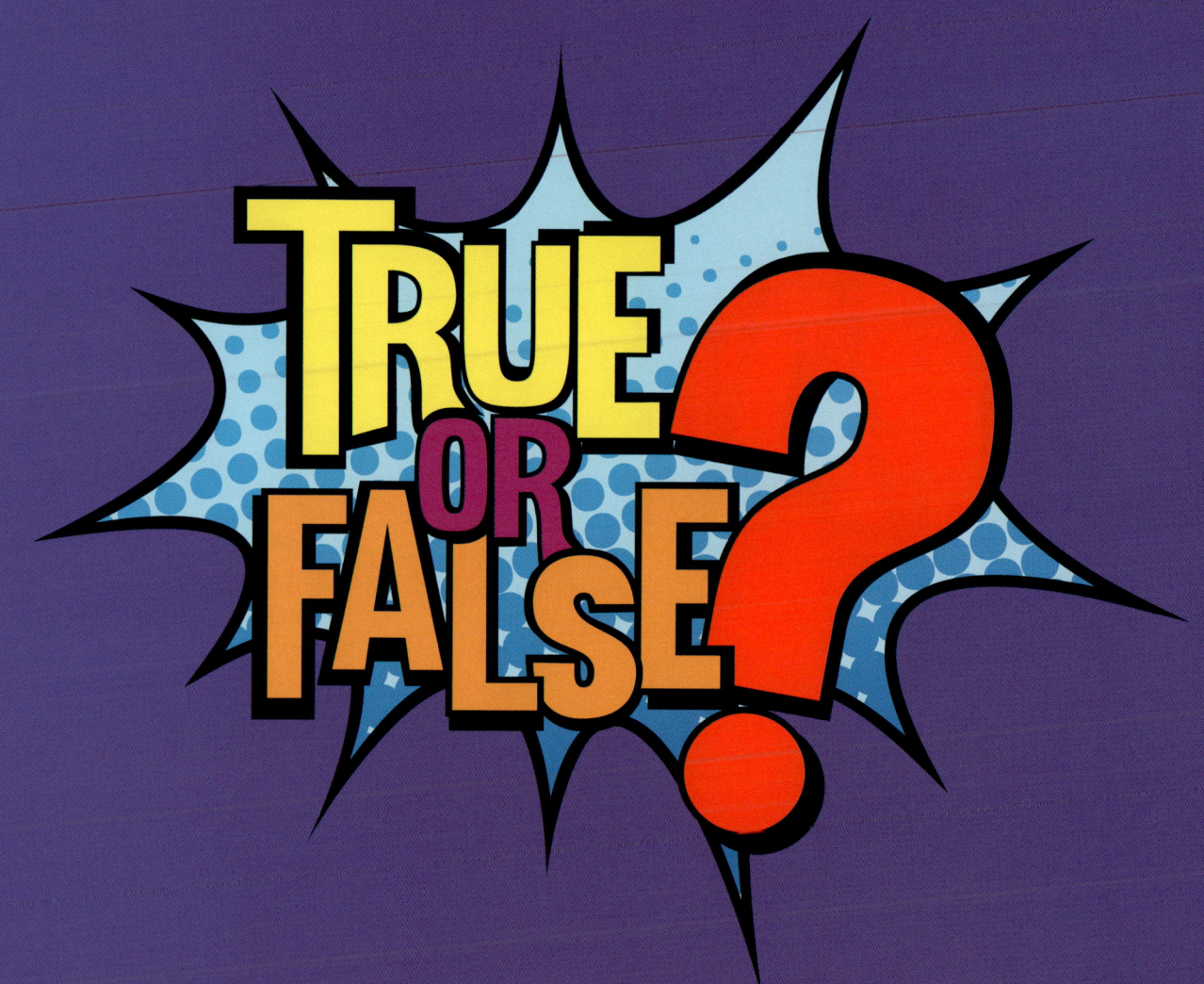

Legend has it that at Woodchester Mansion in England, spirits tickle your toes when you enter. When you laugh, you wake more spirits!

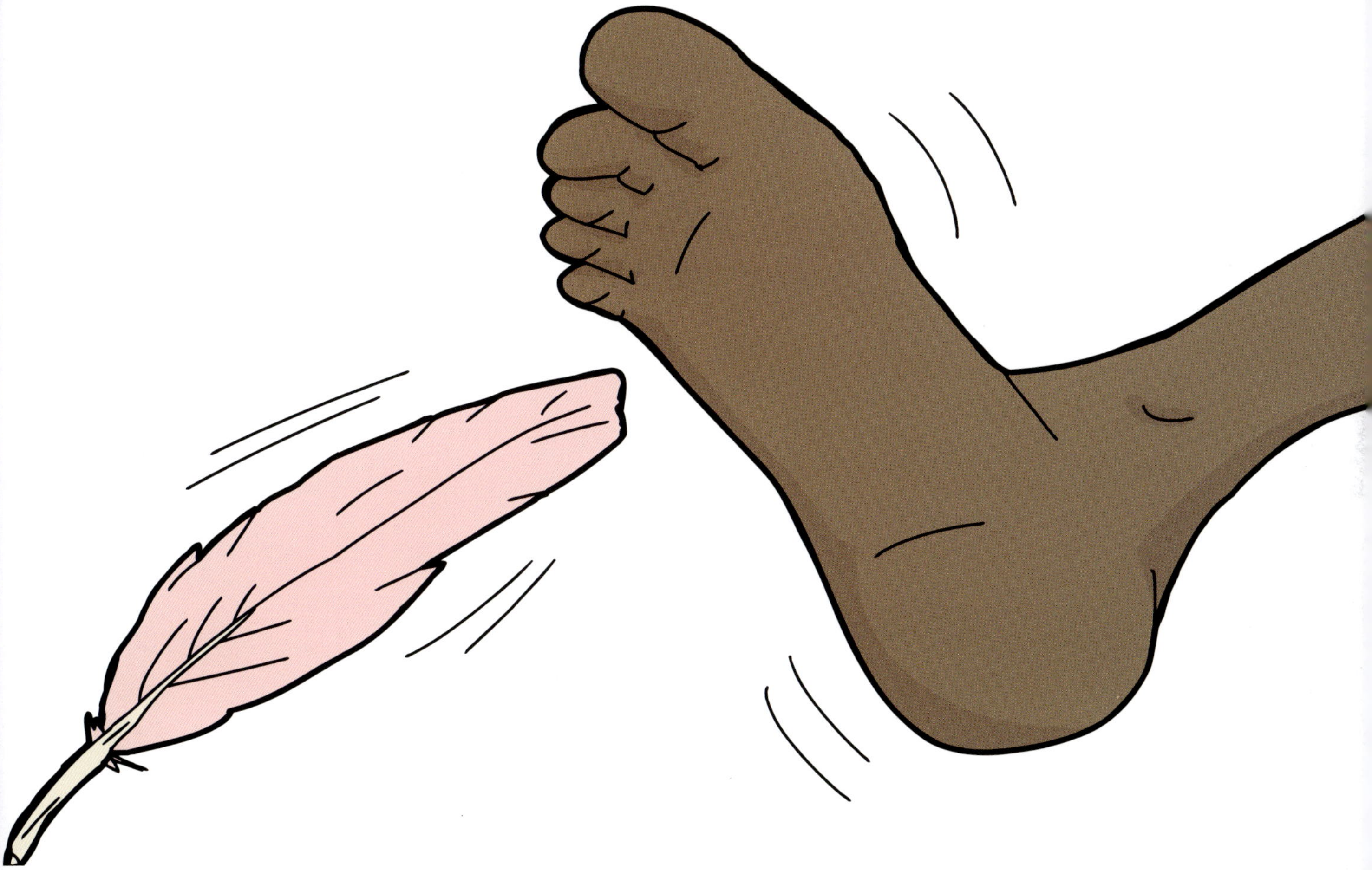

# FALSE!

But people claim spirits pull their hair. *Ouch!* Other people say they see floating coffins and headless horses. What a nightmare!

A *séance (SAY ahns)* is when you say a dead person's name 30 times in a row. If you do, the ghost of the dead person will disappear.

A séance is a meeting at which people try to speak to the dead. The spirit of the dead person supposedly shows its presence by making rapping sounds, by moving objects in the room, or by speaking through a person who claims to communicate with the dead. Watch out for the flying lamp!

# True or False?

**A medium is a person who claims to communicate with the dead.**

# TRUE!

**Mediums often try to talk to the dead at séances. (Mediums come in many sizes.)**

A Ouija *(WEE juh* or *WEE jee)* board is a kind of tool you can make to defend yourself against ghosts.

A Ouija board is a device that is supposed to allow people to talk with spirits. People gather around a board with alphabet letters and numbers printed on it. They place their fingers on a small pointer. The spirit supposedly answers questions by moving the pointer to "yes" or "no" on the board or by spelling out words by moving from letter to letter.

# TRUE OR FALSE?

When the ghost at Monte Cristo Homestead in Australia appears, she carries a silver boomerang.

When people visit this house in the town of Junee in New South Wales, they claim to see a ghost walking through the rooms. When she appears, she brings an ice-cold chill and carries a large silver cross. (A *boomerang* is a curved, flat tool used for hunting or sport.)

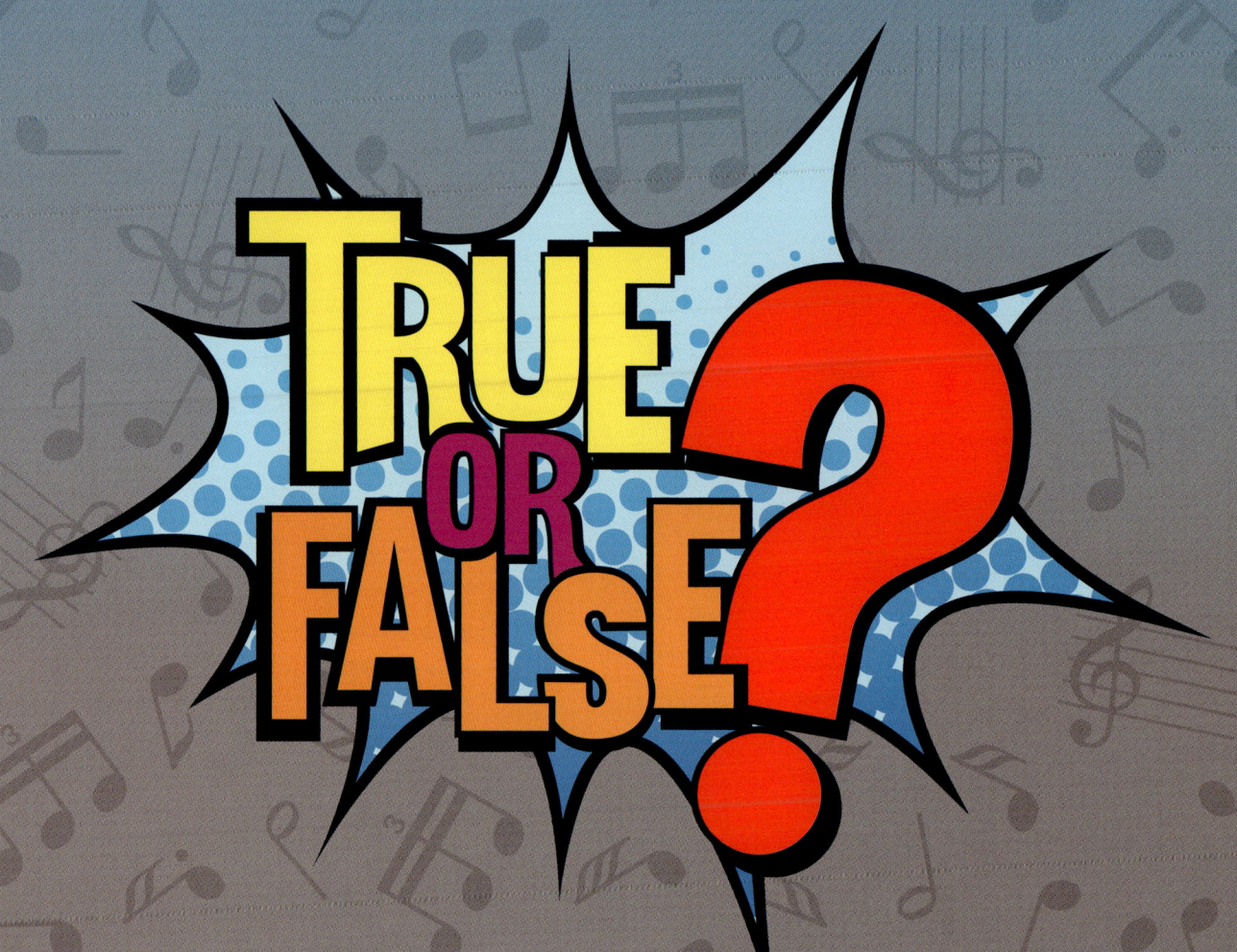

# True or False?

If you believe in the ghost story of el Silbón *(ehl seel bon)* of Venezuelan folklore, you should especially beware of someone whistling the musical scale *(do-re-mi-fa-so-la-ti-do)* right next to you!

According to the legend of el Silbón, also known as "The Whistler," when the whistling sounds close, there's no danger, and the ghost is far away. But when the whistling sounds distant, it means el Silbón is nearby! It is also said that hearing the whistling foretells your own death! A clanking sound is another sign that el Silbón is near. It's the bones of his victims rattling in his sack!

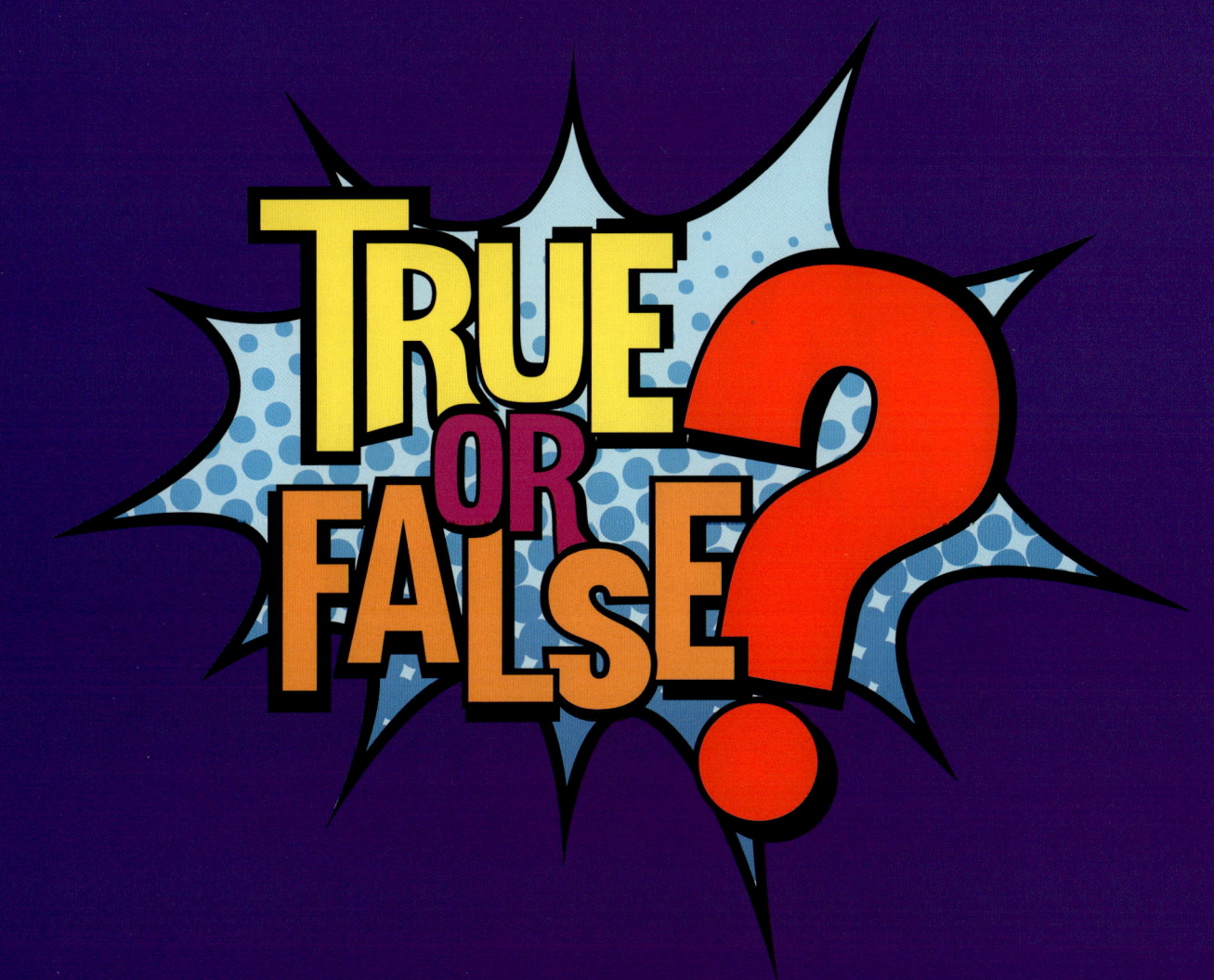

A ghost town is a town inhabited by ghosts.

A ghost town is a town that nobody lives in anymore. All the buildings are empty, and many are falling down. Ghost towns are usually more than 100 years old and have been empty for a very long time. You can find ghost towns in the western United States, Alaska, and Canada. In China, there are hundreds of ghost towns that have apartments, skyscrapers, and public art—but no people.

# DID YOU KNOW...

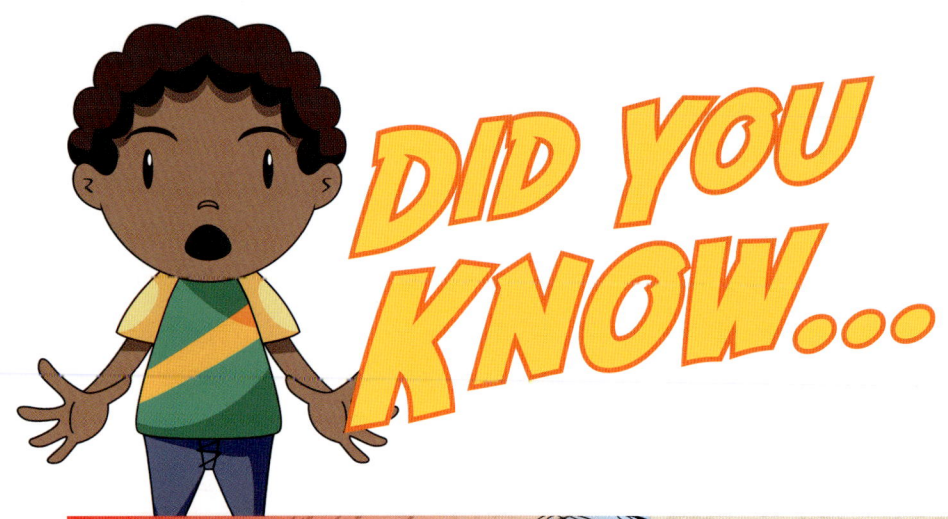

In Victorian England, it was popular for upper-class ladies to hold séances in their parlors. While speaking to the spirits, they **drank tea and ate crumpets.**

British educator Eleanor Sidgwick was the **original female** ghostbuster.

**The American magician Harry Houdini** became known for his great escapes and for exposing mediums as frauds. **He died on Halloween in 1926.**

According to German folklore, all living creatures have **an identical spirit.** The identical spirit is called ***a doppelgänger.***

Some ghost hunters believe that Albert Einstein's scientific laws prove that **ghosts exist.**

# Index

**A**

Australian ghost legend, 80–83

**B**

bathroom ghosts, 52–55
Black Death, 56–59
boomerangs, 80–83

**C**

China, ghost towns in, 90
*Christmas Carol, A* (Dickens), 18–19
Churchill, Winston, 26
Coleridge, Samuel Taylor, 35
Coolidge, Grace, 26

**D**

Danish ghost legend, 28–31
Dickens, Charles, 18–19
doppelgängers, 93
Dracula legend, 51

**E**

Edison, Thomas, 44–47
Einstein, Albert, 93
England
   mansion ghosts in, 64–67
   séances in, 92

**F**

*Flying Dutchman, The* (opera), 35
Flying Dutchman (ship), 34–35

**G**

German folklore, 93
ghost(s)
   Abraham Lincoln's, 24–27
   American Southwest legend about, 60–63
   as harmful, spiteful spirits, 16–19
   as sheet-draped figures, 12–15
   as spirits of dead people, 4–7
   Australian legend about, 80–83
   Danish legend about, 28–31
   Edison's wish to find, 44–47
   English legend about, 64–67
   famous ship as, 32–35
   ghost town, 89–92
   ghostbusters and, 40–43, 92
   Halloween as time to see, 20–23
   Jackson's story about, 36–39
   Japanese folk tales about, 52–55
   mediums and, 72–75
   Ouija boards and, 76–79
   Romanian forest legend about, 48–51
   Scandinavian legend about, 56–59
   scientific proof of, 8–11, 93
   séances and, 68–71
   Venezuelan legend about, 84–87
ghost towns, 89–92
ghostbusters, 40–43, 92
gjenganger, 31

## H

Halloween, 20–23, 93
Hanako-san, 55
*Haunting of Hill House, The* (Jackson), 36–39
Hoia Baciu Forest, 50–51
Houdini, Harry, 93

## J

Jackson, Shirley, 36–39
Japanese folk tales, 52–55
Johnson, Lady Bird, 26
Junee, New South Wales, 82–83

## K

kitchen ghosts, 60–63

## L

Lincoln, Abraham, 24–27
Llorona, La, 62–63

## M

Marley, Jacob, 18–19
mediums, 72–75, 93
Monte Cristo Homestead, 80–83

## O

Ouija boards, 76–79

## P

paranormal investigators, 43
Pesta, 59
plague, 59

## R

"Rime of the Ancient Mariner, The" (Coleridge), 35
Romania, haunted forest in, 48–51
Roosevelt, Eleanor, 26

## S

Scandinavian legend, 56–59
science, 8–11, 93
Scrooge, Ebenezer, 18–19
séances, 68–71, 92
shrouds, 15
Sidgwick, Eleanor, 92
Silbón, el, 84–87
"spirit phone," 47

## T

Transylvania, 51

## U

unidentified flying objects (UFO's), 51

## V

Venezuelan legend, 84–87

## W

Wagner, Richard, 35
whistling by ghost, 84–87
White House, 24–27
Wilhelmina, Queen of the Netherlands, 26
Woodchester Mansion, 64–67

# Acknowledgments

| | |
|---|---|
| Cover: | © Indigo Fish/Shutterstock; © Fpmx/Shutterstock |
| 5-17 | © Shutterstock |
| 19 | © Metro-Goldwyn-Mayer |
| 20-42 | © Shutterstock |
| 45 | Library of Congress |
| 46-56 | © Shutterstock |
| 58 | *Plague travels around the country* (1904), pencil, watercolor, charcoal and crayon on paper by Theodor Kittelsen; Nasjonalmuseet (Getty Images) |
| 60-81 | © Shutterstock |
| 83 | Framton Goodman (licensed under CC BY-ND 2.0) |
| 84-91 | © Shutterstock |
| 92 | © Shutterstock; *Eleanor Sidgwick* (1889), oil on canvas by Sir James Jebusa Shannon; University of Cambridge |
| 93-96 | © Shutterstock |